M000116315

Lilies from America

Also by Carmen Bugan

Poetry
Crossing the Carpathians (Carcanet/Oxford*Poets*, 2004)
The House of Straw (Shearsman Books, 2014)
Releasing the Porcelain Birds (Shearsman Books, 2016)

In translation
Sulla Soglia Della Dimenticanza (Edizioni Kolibris, 2014)
Den Begravda Skrivmaskinen (Wahlström & Widstrand, 2014)
Zakopać Maszynę do Pisania: Dzieciństwo pod Okiem Securitate
                                    (Wydawnictwo Czarne, 2015)
Prose
Burying the Typewriter: Childhood Under the Eye of the Secret Police
        (Picador, UK / Graywolf, USA, 2012)
Seamus Heaney and East European Poetry in Translation: Poetics of Exile
        (Legenda/Maney Publishing, 2013)

Carmen Bugan

Lilies from America

New & Selected Poems
2004-2019

Shearsman Books

First published in the United Kingdom in 2019 by
Shearsman Books
50 Westons Hill Drive
Emersons Green
BRISTOL
BS16 7DF

Shearsman Books Ltd Registered Office
3 – 1 St. James Place, Mangotsfield, Bristol BS16 9JB
(this address not for correspondence)

www.shearsman.com

ISBN 978-1-84861-673-8

Copyright © Carmen Bugan, 2004, 2014, 2016, 2019

The right of Carmen Bugan to be identified as the author of this
work has been asserted by her in accordance with
the Copyrights, Designs and Patents Act of 1988.
All rights reserved.

ACKNOWLEDGEMENTS

This selection of poems comes from the following collections, with the
permission of the publishers: *Crossing the Carpathians* (Oxford Poets/Carcanet,
2004); *The House of Straw* (Shearsman Books, 2014); *Releasing the Porcelain
Birds* (Shearsman Books, 2016). Particular thanks are due to Carcanet Press for
granting permission to reprint. Several of the new poems have been published
in *Shearsman* magazine, *The Irish Times, Big Scream,* and *Oxford Magazine.*

I thank the Centre for the Study of the Archives of the Securitate (CNSAS) in
Bucharest for giving me access to the archive of surveillance documents on my
family and for reassuring me that I can publish these documents. I also thank
my family for allowing me to publish the excerpts from our archive that appear
in the current book in my literal translation. The language of the translations
reflects the secret-police-speak in the original files: I made no effort to correct
the grammar or improve the flow of the transcripts. I am grateful to Lucy
Newlyn and the Hall Writers' Forum at St. Edmund's Hall, Oxford University,
for reading and commenting on early drafts of some of these poems. I thank
Kelvin Corcoran for his keen and generous editorial feedback on the poems and
I thank Tony Frazer at Shearsman for his continuous publishing support: none
of this would have been possible without their commitment to the poems.

Contents

from *The House of Straw* 2014

from *Releasing the Porcelain Birds* 2016

New Poems 2019

For my children, Alisa and Stefano

Lilies from America

In memory of Tanti Saftica

You shall have white lilies
Like the ones you grew all your life
In your front garden.

Over three nights of wake,
On your final walk through the village,
And at the last church service,

When you will leave your place
In the choir, and your living candle
Will be blown out, moved to the candelabra

At the altar, where the candles for the dead
Weep in sand, you shall have
Madonna lilies next to you.

I ordered them from America.
They didn't put the phone to your ear
So I could say I love you once more.

They said there was little breath left in you
And the drops of water they squeezed
On your rigid lips, spilled over.

You shall have white lilies that grow
In glass houses this bitter January,
For the scent of spring that will no longer

Return to you, but will arrive to me
Without you in it. You are with the angels now,
Oh, you are with the angels,

And your body is laid out in the front room
With your hands holding the cross,
Wearing the black winter coat.

We are so far away, we who left
Thirty years ago this year, and visited
Twice, when you touched us

As if we were dreams about to vanish.
Your last words to me were, "I know
I will not see you again, I know."

I knew you did not believe me, but
I am learning we must sometimes
Make promises we cannot keep.

This morning I sent you white lilies
And a wreath of white roses, for the time
When stars will blink above your grave.

from

Crossing the Carpathians

(2004)

In the silent country

When the hens climbed the tree to sleep and the dog was let loose in
        the yard,
When their children went to bed, she covered the windows
In the doors with towels, and hung the yellow blanket over the curtain rod.

He went outside, around the farthest corner of the house, dug the typewriter
From its hole, then from the garage brought a stack of papers hidden
Behind tools in a box. They locked the room.

Both sat at the large oak table and put on gloves to hide fingerprints.
Each night, one by one, hundreds of pages darkened with communal
        demands:
Hot water, electricity, freedom of speech, freedom to worship, freedom
        to assemble.

Their arms smelled of fresh ink. The room was the sound of struck keys
Between two breaths. Not one star looked inside, but the wind joined
        the hush
Of shuffled paper. Before the rooster broke the news of dawn, he put
        the typewriter

In its white crate and buried it in the ground at the back of the house.
She stacked the leaflets in boxes with beans on top —same beans for months,
Wrinkled and dry like old thumbs. With the towels back in the closet

And the blanket down, the room returned to order, quiet and dark like
        the street.
They kissed the children in their sleep. Posing as farmers, they left for
        distant towns
Where he filled mailboxes while she watched for informers and police.

Hues of mornings changed with seasons, but the early sun
Spilled light over his face, over her hands holding the map.
At times, when they stopped to wash out the sleep with cold water, he
        could see

The dark of her eyes. Fists met at the market and in the store,
Churches were demolished, and no one said a word:
Those waiting in eternal lines, or those who saw the crosses kneel

In the rubble of saints and chalices. When they slept, words
Rose from the stacks and they breathed them as they were on paper:
Hot water, electricity, freedom of speech, freedom to worship, freedom
        to assemble.

They retraced in dreams each step: typewriter in the ground,
Papers behind the tools, gloves in the cupboard, the dark entryways
Where the words went, someone looking at them through a crack in
        the door.

Every night the words replaced them – *her pale skin, her long brown hair.*
They whispered into the sleep of others, in the silent country.

Portrait of a family

When the strangers walked into the house,
Took the paintings off the walls, and
Sealed off the rooms with red wax,

Part of this poem listened in a hospital. A woman's milk
Fed the words she couldn't say into her child's mouth.
For seven months the strangers stayed in the house.

Someone tied the hands of the man
Who inflamed the centre of the capital with protest,
While they took the paintings off the walls.

A few lines cowered in the grass, outside the windows,
With the neighbors who watched the girl answering questions
To the strangers who settled into the house.

And yet someone followed her sister on the streets
And photographed her pure black eyes,
Unsuspecting in the paintings on the walls.

Now that the strangers have left the house,
The poem would like to know:
Can it place once more the paintings on the walls,

Will the son tell the secrets of his mother's milk,
Will the handcuffs come off the man's hands,
Will the girl stop answering questions,
Will her sister burn the photographs?

The demonstration

I remember the night my father left
Filling a bag with leaflets and tying the placards
On top of the car: 'We Demand the Trial of the Ceaușescu Family
For Crimes Against Humanity, Usury and Economic Downfall.'

I complained about the boiled cabbage.
Please come and lock the gates. Tell them nothing.
I fell asleep on the kitchen sofa listening to Radio Free Europe.

In Bucharest he placed the placards on the front and back of the car.
He drove through traffic on the main street.
People came out of the stores shouting.
Buses and trams stopped, emptied, let him pass.

He threw leaflets with the left hand, drove with the right hand.
Ah, it was glorious! The flag of his country draped round his chest.
The portrait of the dictator decorated with black ribbons.

In a hospital, Dad's only son was born –
Mother held his bluish body wrapped in white cloth
At the window.

Thousands saw him being pulled from the car,
Watched him between armed soldiers.
None of his countrymen said a word.

Fertile ground

I was pruning tomato plants when they came to search
For weapons in our garden;
They dug the earth under the chickens, bell peppers,
Tiny melons, dill, and horseradishes.

I cried over sliced eggplants
Made one with the dirt,
Over freshly-dug earth and morning glories.

Their shovels uncovered bottles
With rusted metal caps – sunflower cooking oil
My father kept for 'dark days,' purchased in days equally dark.
Their eyes lit – everyone got a bottle or two –
A promise for their families' meals.

And when the oil spilled on the ground, shiny over crushed tomatoes,
They asked me about weapons we might have kept.
'Oil,' I said: 'You eat and live.
This alone makes one dangerous.'

The first visit

The family went inside cement walls
In the centre of the town,
Stood inside metal gates
In the centre of the prison,
And waited.

Hours swelled
Like the shadows of passing black trucks
Loaded with criminals.

When they finished shaving him,
After they covered the wounds on his head with a cap,
There was a rumble of chains and keys.
His wife and children were taken to the visiting room:
'Twenty minutes,' the guard said.

Twenty minutes in August each year
Twenty minutes –
A mouth full of suffering,
Words swollen by microphones
Sank into the thick wall of glass
Between us.

Through two rooms, through two square holes in the walls
The little boy said:
'Daddy, I thought I'd bring you some apples.'

The divorce

Before they brought him to the courtroom, they gave
him three apples: 'Your wife sent you these.'
He cradled each apple in the cup of his hands,
The smoothness of their skin became the cheeks of each child.

Inside the courthouse there was a quiet opening and closing of doors.
A crowd of people was chanting his name under the windows.
When the door opened, I saw his bare feet in brown shoes.

His children held each other tight against the wall.
Their breaths, white with cold, were rising towards the ceiling.
They listened for the voices of their parents.

When the divorce was over, he was allowed to see them:
They kissed his chained hands, promised to be good, let their tears fall
On his prison uniform with his own, all three of them burying him.
How I wished we could hide him with our bodies and take him home!

The Securitate peeled us off him.
But we were the apple seeds left to grow
In the sound of his chains on the cement floor.

Stories for the night

The family sat in the kitchen again for the first time in years;
The white table filled with plates of polenta, meat, and goat's cheese,
Glasses of water halfway empty, a tiny red carnation in a vase at the centre.

The father smiled sadly at his children from the head of the table:
'Don't ask me things before going to bed,
These are not your grandmother's stories.'

He dropped his hands to his knees and looked at each of them:
'One night they woke me up and beat me,
The fat officer hit me over the left ear; I can't hear well since.

They tied me up and hung me on the wall, my hands chained behind
        my back,
Toes barely touched the floor. I stood there for thirty-six hours.
One of the three men from my cell died:

We propped him up, told the guards he was alive
So we could have his bread and water.
After some time he smelled bad, rats were eating too much of him,
And we gave him away.

A man tied to a wheel
A man pinned to a wall
Shards of glass in our soup,
That's how it was there.'

Taking leave

You take my hand between rough fingers
And we cross the ocean on the map to America.
I think of days left for you to have wine and walnuts,
To feed pigeons in the yard with corn grains,
Of one more spring when you will walk the palms
Of your hands over the yellow bed of tulips.

Sitting on a chair in front of the house
Even through the haze of Alzheimer's you know
This leave-taking is the final one – and how are we
To stretch this moment so far that it will last a lifetime?
We, who go, stand in front of you waiting for blessings
From your blue, confused, wet eyes.

'Make me an altar before you go,
In the kitchen, on top of the cupboard.
On your grandmother's crochet tablecloth,
With grapes made of fabric, put the icons of St Mary and St Nicholas.
Then light the oil lamp, my child. After you leave, I'll pray for you there.'

Around us, neighbors and family weep with the weeping of funerals,
Two dumb girls plead with us not to go,
The crowd is astonished at their garbled words.

And only when Mother starts pounding on Dad's chest
Overcome with the madness of leaving everything,
You stand up: 'It's your duty to go,' you say.
The crowd walks us to the gate, the car, a dog barks,
Birds sing. It is October.
Alone, you are left in the chair, warmed only by the sun.

The train station at the border

At Moravita the last officer opened each suitcase
And turned each pocket inside out.
He felt the lining of coats, his thievish hands
Fondled and fondled.

It was words he took, words
Hidden between socks and underclothes in a blue notebook:
Condemned for propaganda against the socialist regime
This day of September 1983.
While passengers watched, the family was escorted out
Onto the stone platform where the day woke up cold.

All day and all night,
They sat on a stone bench in a stone station.
The father was angry with the final body search.
His face, flushed and desperate,
Tried to regain dignity as he stepped
From the stone office into the stone hall.
Through small windows
October went on coloring trees.
The army hounds paced around the station with the soldiers.
The little boy never said he was hungry,
His mother made a bed for him
Out of suitcases and winter coats;
There he slept without dreams.
His parents and two sisters
Paced inside the stone station at the border
Without a glass of water, without a word.

Grand Rapids, Michigan

Father repeats his own name aloud as if to remember it:
Sheepskin coat, blood-shot eyes, one suitcase,
He carries his age and his language on his tongue.

Mother gathers us around her:
I still see on her face the green lights on the platform in Bucharest,
The arm of the conductor lifting to *Go*!

When we crossed the frontier
We drank quietly from a flask of plum brandy:
I still don't know what each of us was thinking.

Someone carries a sign with our name written on it,
We don't know him but embrace him
And let him drive us through driving snow.

In exile

…and I've been searching for home
ever since the train whistled in darkness.

Home

In last night's dream gladioli grew wild around the house,
Queens-of-the-night crashed through walls,
And the remains of the windowsills were overtaken
By tall while lilies and blue irises.
The roses we grew for preserves strangled the front door.

I was sitting next to the poplar grown through the roof
When I saw a man hanging smoked fish under the eaves.
My grandparents were having a meal of bread, onion, and water;
They were talking about bringing the corn to the mill,
And threshing the beanstalks in the yard.

From the beans, the smell of summer.
I saw the sticks we made out of oak branches,
I remembered how we sat in the circle,
The dust from the stalks as we beat them –
Something like the sound of galloping horses.

They carried on with the meal. Then they sifted wheat.
I saw them walk right past me. They loaded the cart.
And I thought I heard my name in the throat of a gladiolus.

For Sorin

It was never a festival
Of chrysanthemums,
Holding each other in parks.

Never an oath on St Mary's painting,
Ready to abandon words,
Rolling in the grass at night.

Never love-making –
The still wet hair,
Cards I sent from Trieste.
Never building a house.

But I imagined we'd live in the mountains
With peasants, getting drunk,
Chopping wood in winters,
Riding horses in summers,
Betting on the weather.

At her funeral

for my grandmother

Villagers dressed in black lay bridges of cloth
From the living room to the carriage,
And walk the coffin on their shoulders,
Over the threshold,
Over the bed of chrysanthemums
She had looked at in the early mornings.

The mourners put their hands together
Under the black ribbons above the doors,
And sing of her eyebrows turning into moss,
Her eyes turning into violets,
Her bones turning into flutes.

The priest leads the cortège to the church
With the book and three boys carrying scarf-flags.
They stop at every street corner
To make prayers of return into humid earth.

Here, in the horse-drawn carriage,
She is a bride crossing the gate to the cemetery
Behind a trail of incense and songs,
A wooden cross, and a box filled with bread.

Hundreds of oak leaves whisper in the sun.
Her soul, like a vapor,
Joins the afternoon light
From mounds of flowers and lit candles.

I drink with you

for my aunt Sáftica

When you knew that I was leaving
You bought me a pair of red shoes;
I left them in Florence with the memory of your hands.
You were unsure when you said, 'So you'll dance and forget.'
October was pale in a bouquet of chrysanthemums.
For every year that I was gone you buried in the ground
One crimson bottle of wine. I never knew this –
How you felt when you gathered the sweetness of autumn,
And hoped that its magic would call me back.
Now I touch the corners of your black scarf,
The white hair of your widow-braids. I kiss your hands,
Which rest on the wine-stained tablecloth.

Crossing the Carpathians with you

for my mother

Mountains and us clothed
In soft white fog,
Suddenness of cliffs.

You and I carve walking sticks,
Bursts of sun dust
Thousands of yellow and violet flowers.

Red and white polka-dot
Mushrooms among trees,
Strong smell of ferns and cones.

Stones in pots on our backs
Warnings to black bears,
We gather forget-me-nots.

Distant curves
Of snow and peaks
In the white of the moon.

Shepherds' rain fast and thin;
We empty the boots of water,
A bear licks out pots.

I know what it means to go
Anywhere with you: you are
The moss on which I sleep.

Sleeping apple

I want to sleep the sleep of the apples
                                        Lorca

She dreams of how constellations
Of apples turn in their sleep
Towards stars in the silence
Of the orchard.

I know she dreams:
She glows in the basket
Nestled among blushing sisters.

This spring

While she uproots blooming irises from the backyard,
Where they grow for no one,
And brings them to the flower bed next to the road,
Gusts of wind and sun blind and lose her.

She digs with her fingers to feel the reality of soil,
Not as harsh as the pain of letting go,
Or as otherworldly as the bird's nest which
She knocks over with her shoulder.

But she looks for that softness and warmth
That will be a sort of home – after death.
The father wobbles in his sandals towards the flowers
Thinking of the image of his heart on the monitor –
A muscle the size of his fist flickering with the weight of light.

She plants a row of irises on the side of house and he smiles
At fragrant violet and white petals unfolding:
'In July we'll have gladioli and next year
Let's get lots of colors, lots of colors.'

She tells him that the peonies and geraniums and roses and tiger lilies
Grow so strongly, it must be a good sign: he will get better, she says.

This is the hour when there is only time for
Delicate colors around the grey house, the locust trees in the yard
From which they take armfuls of blossoms and bring them in,
And fill the rooms with the white scent of blown spring.

For my father

You sign your full name with a stick on the freshly poured
Path of cement: the end of the last letter returns to your first name
In the wet dust. Around, a slew of peonies
Hurry to bloom before the bluebells, before you plant them.

You surprise me with dill seeds from Grandmother
That you kept since our last trip home.
You brought her in this soil and now we are together
Through plants we touched in different countries.

Remember? A cart full of red and white grapes at the head
Of our vineyard, red wine pressed years before,
Goat's cheese and tomatoes spread under the oak tree,
And horses let loose for children, whose voices ripened the earth.

*

I have the picture in which you crossed yourself in front of St Mary's
        icon at Vatra.
It was the first week of chemotherapy when we had the service with
Seven candles and seven prayers and seven readings from the Gospels.
Seven times we walked to the altar where the priest painted crosses with
        holy oil

On our cheeks, on our foreheads, and the backs of our hands. For we
        must sin
With our minds, hurt others with our hands, and carry our shame on
        our faces.
So we try to redeem ourselves with our minds, and hands, and clean
        our cheeks.
I look at your pale profile, at your balding head in front of those candles,
And ask what the mother in red and her child in white,
Carefully placed in the whitest of wood frames, will do for you.
We cried with you: Mother, I, and a congregation of exiles

Dreaming their own into the smoke of the censer.

*

We are small gardens in strange places, small voices –
Prayers weakening with age and heavy accents hammering wrong
        syllables:
Does God understand us in English or our own language still?

You choose the path with handwriting that marks your name and year,
And I carry your garden in my head, along with the memory of you
        and Mother
Embracing on the doorstep the day we received the news:
In the months to come, what binds us is the most silent of prayers,
        unuttered still.

Flight dream

At three in the afternoon I slung
The hiking boots over the rucksack
And left Oxford in a pool of June sun.

Crowds of motorcycles in Poole Harbour,
Through narrow streets, boats and seagulls:
Half industrial, half dreamy, this is not my place.

Ten o'clock finds me tense in a yellow room
Caught dreaming between two islands,
Or rather imagining my head in your palms.

Handfast Point

After I saw the peacock on the sand,
Proud and dispossessed
Of its blue by the sunlit tide,

I thought of you, miles on,
Past the pottery beach,
After reeds, willows, and birch:

You, of course, are the one
Who would understand
Cursing and releasing

The heart, white chalk,
Like the rock of Old Harry,
With the blue hand of sea.

Black Head Ledges

This is the safe white room with a sea window
And rain after sun, a badger among bluebells.
My hosts tell me of their travels over *palinka*

And Hungarian wine from the Valley of Egar.
This is how I arrived here: when the clouds
Came like premonitions over the Black Head Ledges,

I lost faith and pressed on, weight on mind and body.
Then the sun returned and shone over Osmington
More like a lighthouse beam than a promise.

The distance between the path and the edge,
Sure footing and falling under weight of backpack
Opened the hours between cliffs and sky – in long silence.

Windspit

Beyond the Dancing Ledge the salt breeze widens
And whispers into caves, but its sound at times
Hurls itself underground, then rises just as a hum

To where my feet, blistered and determined,
Meet the old path. I search again with
Sea-tasting hair in dry mouth –

The weight of winspit, wishspit, windspit
Love which opens to love of sorts:
Pub table, drenched clothes, white cliffs;

At the end of today's walk over the sound
Of sea under the path, sudden soft
Explosions through gaps and tunnels, underfoot.

At the window

Wet leaf slapped itself against the glass,

You turned directly to my mouth in the crowd

Then slid down

Lowered yourself to my waist

Leaving the mark of its width along the window.

Until, transparent, I bore your kiss.

Past solitude

Breakfast of mackerel at a table facing foxgloves,
Then luck of low tide: so I slid on boulders,
Threaded a small footpath through mud, all the while

Balancing backpack and weight on boots.
When I thought that river Char opens its mouth into the sea,
I regretted the blackness of my words to you,

And hoped that tides would keep cleaning them from me.
From Charmouth to Chideock I walked on the motor-way,
And from there to Seatown, thatch-roofed cottages and fields of lambs.

All the way to West Bay it was cliff-top to bottom-of-hill,
Deep green under a grey sky and breath-labour.
I am a snail, moving slowly, watchful and regretful at times.

Here, at the window, after gravel beach which led
To golden cliffs in which I stuck my fingers at the end
Of solitude, I paint myself with the dusk of Sunday.

Abbotsbury

Eype Mouth, Burton Freshwater, Burton Beach, Cogden Beach,
And yellow, yellow rape patches folded in soft hills which
Kneel, golden and wrinkled, towards the speaking sea.

Then Chesil Beach and boots and blue pool surprising
The eye with its stillness – rhythm of gravel walk and waves,
An afternoon of intense heat and colors in the heart of silence.

Imagine a bride, wild with waiting for first night:
She throws handfuls of roses in hidden valleys,
Where they take root in the stone of houses.

That is Abbotsbury. She goes to pray
At St Nicolas's Abbey up on the hill and buries her past
In the hip of the cemetery which faces the Fleets.

And she raises a thousand swans now nesting,
And she turns her flock of lambs in the sunlight.
I walk over her body, dream-eyed.

Evening

for my grandfather

The stork returns from the river
With a snake in its beak –

Wing-shadow and wing-flap and then
He stands on one foot in his tree.

The hens go slowly blind and head to sleep,
Quinces light up crepuscular,

And I am old enough to come looking for you
In the back garden at the stove, amid fireflies.

Dinner is always a formal affair with you:
Dark suit, white shirt and tie,

Walnut-oil in your hair.
So you sweat under August

And under your black hat. Your old hands
Tame a fire of twigs and cornstalks.

I imagine you in a painting – tall at the stove
In the garden; fire, polenta

Settled in simmer, eggs, milk in froth –
Framed by a purple sky and rows of quinces.

You stand next to a tree with a stork at the top.
I step into the canvas, a child with uncombed hair,

To stand in the dirt next to you:
A dusty statue with the bluest eyes.

For my mother and sister

When she was a child, and there was a drought,
She dressed the cob of the corn in yellowed leaves,
Made overcoats out of rags to clothe the corn dolls,
And threw them in the weakened river,
Then ran along the riverbank with the other children
Chanting prayers for rain.

That was long ago. Last night she remembered the chant
And sang it while she held my hand, but I don't
Remember the words now, for one never remembers
Things received abundantly –

'Did it rain?' I asked her. I pictured a girl with brown hair,
She, orphan at three, growing along the river and
Cornfields. 'I don't know,' she said, 'but I liked the magic.'

This morning she left with a suitcase – rain
Fell over the Broad Street all through midday –
She and the other one, my dark-eyed sister,
Who has a touch for driving away the pain
Just like that.

I stood at the window and waved, blessed with their strength
For there and then I could finally say: 'Let health and fortune be
With you. I left you across the seas, and you came to me
From the heart of love, and gave generously.'
They walked along the current of the empty morning street,
Carrying miracles with them.

from

The House of Straw

(2014)

Twenty years

The horizon was the blue spine of a book,
Its pages frozen sand, iced-over waves
And I, still unwashed of airplane fumes,
Day's sweat, bitterness of instant coffee,
Went knee-deep in water, where I first wrote
Out of my life the tangled algae of the Black Sea.

Who can see ahead on that first day when
You awake without a country, a house,
In a well-meaning stranger's bed, your
Host speaking to you in an alien language?
I ate the food she served with trembling hands,
It was snowing outside, warm inside.

The following year I erased the birds: woodpecker,
Sparrow, grandfather's pigeons, and the faithful stork.
In their place I wrote the hawks that scanned
The dunes of Sleeping Bear, crows, hummingbirds,
Red cardinals singing
In the too-large garden of our new house.

But on this page I am leaning against lighthouses,
While cherry orchards grow to the tip of Leelanau,
Tree roots in water. They swish over whitened-out
Cornfields of my childhood. All things I wanted to forget
Crowd in-between the lines I spent years writing:
Four languages, ambitions, homesickness, dispersed friends.

*

Today it is twenty years since that evening at the airport,
When in blinding snow people we had not seen
Were waiting for us. They said I kissed the ground.
Did I kiss the ground? Who can remember this?
We search ourselves through memories,
Or autumn leaves that fall, breaking into something else.

Making the hay mattress

The best part of all that was dancing:
In August, at the summer cleaning,
She threw away mattress and pillows

Stripping our bed to an idea on the empty floor,
Where, with hammer and nails, she reinforced
Wobbly corners of the wooden frame.

Then, in a new white case, we stuffed fresh hay;
After she sealed it, she summoned us to dance
The *hora* on top to even out the surface,

Soften flowers, herbs, and grass.
Barefoot, we took lessons on the mattress:
Stomped our feet, clapped our hands, laughed.

So it was, that till the day she died,
We danced in August, and slept on flowers at night.

Harvesting beans

The garden strewn with dry bean-
Pods rattling on their stems
As we shook them out of sacks
Onto sheets spread on the grass.

Holding thick oak sticks, we sat
In a circle and beat the stalks:
Sending the freckled beans up
Free as heavy raindrops.

Grandfather waited for the wind
With instruments for sifting:
A clean straw rug, a tub-sized
Wooden bowl, and a tin bucket.

That's how he remained
Pictured in my child-mind:
A shadow in the summer breeze,
His back to the orange sun,

Hat pushed to his brow,
Hands lifting a bucket of beans,
Sounding like a downpour
As they fell, cleared of husks.

Harvesting walnuts

Early in October, when our walnut tree
Began to drop a nut or two, here, there,
First letting go of the green husks,
With a *pluck* and a *plump* then a *thump*,

Grandfather carved sticks, thick as our arms;
We climbed the tree to knock down the walnuts:
From between leaves a bitter smell of iodine
Fell. Back on the ground we sat in a circle.

Holding round stones in yellow-stained hands
We cracked walnuts, built leaf castles
Guarded by turtle armies made of husks
And shells, and we learned the colour bitter-green.

The house of straw*

In memory of my grandparents

'In this world the house will be yours
But in the afterlife it shall be mine.'
So, when they were old, they joined
In the ritual of caring for the band
Of gypsies coming through the village,
Looking after parents left by children
At empty hearths. What you give away
Stays with you in eternity,
For heaven or hell will be received
In a familiar bed, at a table you know.

Each built a separate room in the garden;
Walls and floor of new straw rugs,
A bed with a hay mattress draped in cotton,
White pillows, change of clothes,
Soft slippers to walk around the sky,
A table with chairs, a flower tapestry,
A pail filled with water from our well.
For work, each gave away bags of rice
Which needed separating grain by grain,
Beans, a sack of unsifted wheat,
Corn in a wicker basket, and two hens
To lay eggs around the house.
All other time in heaven is leisurely, they said.

*

And then, the afterlife meal:
Onions, rice, fresh tomatoes were sweated
In sunflower oil, then added to minced meat,
Flavored with parsley and dill, some salt,
Ground pepper, an egg for binding up the mixture,
All wrapped in vine leaves stung in brine

And put to simmer all day long.
Grandmother hovered over polenta
With the wooden spoon, while buttermilk,
Aged in earthen jugs, was ready to be poured.

*

When the poor in this life were called
To receive the roofless houses of straw,
Candles were lit to link living day
To other world with the cord of light;
I watched all those hands uniting
On stems of wax held at thresholds,
I saw love eternal, burning at open doors.
Then in his room, my grandfather brought
A flask of wine, set it on the table, and cried.

*This poem describes *grijirea*, a ritual practised around the villages in the Moldavian region of Romania to prepare people for the afterlife.

Acciecati dalla meraviglia
(Blinded by wonder)

Unchanged, the white curtain in the marble hall
Still half-hanging from the fallen rail

A stack of maps the child couldn't reach that first night,
Still on the gray countertop, at the head of stairs,

The same noise from cheap shops, where they sold
Skirts and trinkets to us refugees, emerging, wide-eyed,

From the end of all trail-tracks at Roma Termini, and first
Memory of self with one suitcase, making a right turn

Out of the station. Then finding, as the blind does,
Whispers counting time in the ventricles

Of Santa Maria Maggiore, on each side of the nave,
From confession box to confession box.

To honor the year when we were blinded by wonder here,
I walk through the same streets, revisit ancient ruins.

In a story beginning the year one hundred and six with Trajan,
I, blood of Dacian beekeeper or weapon-clad conqueror,

Shiver in the sun, not knowing what I am, as voices
From across two thousand years collect in my flesh.

At a gathering of refugees

To her it was a row of whitewashed houses
Rising from the sea; she said the whiteness
Appears and vanishes behind crests of waves.

A wooden gate with a blue rope latch
Was mine; and the path between
Pear and quince.

Neither of us named another thing
Or ate, or stayed to warm up; it was as if
We aimed to hide our strangeness.

We both stood among
Those who owned their land, spoke
Of homelands as if they were reachable;

As if she could sail home to take her seat
At the kitchen table, begin kneading her bread.
As if I could just open the gate to my garden.

The names of things

Sunlight in a water bowl on the doorstep,
Then on a pond far from home: *soarele*.

Fire in the terracotta hearth, then
In a pit, outside a tent, thousands of miles away: *focul*.

My Black Sea lulling the shore, then dreams
Of sea waking cheeks with stinging salt: *marea*.

Air encircling the grapes outside the window,
Then gliding with a parachute above a heron: *aerul*.

Soil exhaling after rain through gaps between cherry leaves,
Then crying dirty tears from roots of a fallen birch: *pamintul*.

Mating swans

She stood still in the centre of the lake,
Head high, raised tail, white calligraphy.

He made a clock on the face of water,
Arresting the sun, her gaze, and the reeds.

From the tongue of twelve o'clock he
Bowed before her, a question mark,

And she answered with her own bow,
A question before him: turn following

Turn. When he mounted her,
I called you and we blushed together

Through their dance of coiling necks,
Kissing beaks, beating wings.

At the end, two questions faced each other,
Raising a heart on their bed of water.

We too, that morning, bowed
And drew on our blue cotton sheets.

From the beginning

For Stefano

The river shimmers under the bridge;
Scales on the back of fish.
Broken ice in the pond glitters,
Life grows inside of me, prepares.

Now that I know you are
Moving and growing,
I make one cross with holy oil
On my belly and one on my chest

So we can breathe together,
And borrow dreams from each other:
Me, your unborn imaginings about
World and sun waiting for you;

You, my blood in which I send you
Fresh food and words,
So when you join us here,
By the water, we can talk.

While chasing rainbows

For Alisa

Thirteen months I waited for the right sky
To describe how I felt when you were born,

And here it is, this morning, out of the blue:
White, gray, translucent clouds hang low,

A row of pearls on the soft Jura, so low
You can see the gentle mountain top in clear sunshine

And worry that somehow the sky is going to fall
On earth, leaving Mt. Blanc in opposite direction

Suspended in the air, spoon-like and white,
Like some kind of fault in vision.

And then, a dust of first snow, an apparition,
Suddenly illuminated by a rainbow,

So clear—from St. Jean de Gonville
To Col de la Faucille—I change direction

And we drive straight into it, as if we're
Going through Heaven's Arch. But it's more:

Another rainbow and another, and another yet,
All day rise and paint the mountain air

With the kind of joy that makes me forget where I am
Going and why. And you are crying in the backseat

As babies do, hungry for breast, comfort, and love.
The day when you arrived it was just like that,

One burst of nature happening after another, mid-morning,
Turning the whole morning right around, feet tiptoeing the birthing sky,

And at eleven and one minute you were landed
On my startled chest. I was still waiting to give birth to you.

The coming of winter

Suddenly trees struggle
With weight of fruit; under branches
The earth is red with apples.

Pears reach our shoulders. It is all
But September, I grip the last hours
Of summer; roses are still opening.

Silver maple leaves; gray in my hair.

There

A drop of water on water:

There

a circle opens slowly

this is your life.

Visiting the country of my birth

The tyrant and his wife were exhumed
For proper burial; it is twenty years since
They were shot against a wall in Christmas snow.

*

The fish in the Black Sea are dead. Waves roll them
To the beach. Tractors comb the sand. We stand at water's edge
Whispering, glassy-eyed, throats parched from heat.

Stray dogs howl through nights like choirs
Of mutilated angels, circle around us on hill paths,
Outside gas stations, shops, streets, in parking lots.

Farther, into wilderness, we slow down where horse
And foal walk home to the clay hut by themselves,
Cows cross roads in evenings alone, bells clinking.

People sit on wooden benches in front of their houses,
Counting hours until darkness, while
Shadows of mountains caress their heads.

On through hot dust of open plane, to my village:
A toothless man from twenty years ago
Asks for money, says he used to work for us.

*

I am searching for prints of mare's hooves in our yard
Between stable and kitchen window, now gone
With the time my two feet used to fit inside one hoof.

We sit down to eat on the porch, when two sparrows
Come flying in circles over the table, low and fast, happily!
'My grandparents' souls,' I think aloud, but my cousin says:

'No, the sparrows have nested under eaves, look
Past the grapevine.' Nests big as cupped hands, twigs
And straw. Bird song skids in the air above us.

Into still-remaining rooms no sewing machine,
Or old furniture with sculpted flowers on walnut wood.
No rose bushes climbing window sills, outside.

And here, our water well, a vase of cracked cement. Past
Ghosts of lilac, pear, and quince in the sun-bitten yard I step
On re-imagined hooves, pull the chain, smell wet rust.

Unblemished sky ripples inside the tin bucket,
Cradled in my arms the way I used to hold
Warm goose eggs close to skin so not to break them:

'The earth will remember you,' my grandparents once said.
Here, where such dreams do not come true, I have come
To find hoof-prints as well as signs from sparrows.

from

Releasing the Porcelain Birds

(2016)

We are museums

We have now become museums. The inside of our souls
Was turned out like the lining of coats hung to dry,
And our souls have dried. Out of us came the warm breath
That you see when you blow on a window or in winter air.

Out of our footprints through the town, from the sound
Of us walking around the house, they have made maps.
When we stopped at a shop window, the minutes were noted,
The address and what we looked at were kept on record:

The red dress on a mannequin, empty shelves in a bakery
On Hope, Victory, or People Street. Because we have become
'Objects of observation,' 'targets,' since nothing more has remained
Of the people we were, we are now museums.

On the ground level, where we were closest to the earth, you will find
Our house with garden and fruit trees with sparrows, nightingales
And monarch butterflies. Then came the time of upheaval when birds
Were shooed from branches, where microphones were installed.

The dog was poisoned by informers. The child was recorded
On a tape, when the electricity was on. The end of the girl's first love,
Her angry letters, have rooms of their own, furnished with her mother's
Sympathy: maybe they were kept to indict us for having had feelings?

There are records of us eating sour soup and polenta, drinking linden tea,
Mother knitting sweaters at two in the morning to exchange for eggs
And flour; you will find her sitting on the bed 'alone by herself
Talking to no one for many hours,' framed forever in the state archives.

On the top floor, where we are further up from the earth, you will see us
Trying to escape: the girl asks her father to 'please talk about Kant,'
And he says, 'plan to live without me if I am assassinated.' We are
Museums. I am writing this down so you can come inside us to see.

There are no secrets anyway, everything about us has been recorded:
Night dreams and rage, irony and double-meaning, shopping we did
At the pharmacy, tears on our cheeks, even the illusion that
There might have been *something* we could have kept for ourselves.

February-April 2013

Found in secret police records
In memory of Seamus Heaney who believed that poetry can assuage pain

The dictator released the news of amnesty on his birthday
'To remain in history for his clemency,' Mother said
Not knowing it was her irony that remained preserved:
In our country people starved and friend informed on friend.

In his prison cell my father's jubilation was recorded:
'If I come out at the same time as any of you,
I'll buy a bottle of wine and some ham, that'll last us till home!'
The jailer warned him not to talk about what had happened there.

When Father came out of the train, the state archives say
He knocked on the door of old friends asking to make a call,
And I was the one who answered.
I sent him to Mother at work—she'd wanted to see him first.

(How she spent all the month's salary on stocking the fridge,
And worried about him travelling in the dead of winter
Wearing only his black suit, how she spat on the face of police
The morning of his release, when they asked her to inform on him.)

They walked in the door holding hands, his wrists raw from chains,
He caressed my brother, wanted to know what I have learned at school,
Then went around the house visiting each room; he asked for his shaver
And his radio, the night wore on. The antennae at the top of our house

Transmitted our feelings, the microphones must have blushed
At our words after long silence, the informer outside the window stood
At his post recording 'the atmosphere of joy on the part of children,'
Witnessing those first slow moments when I 'sobbed out loud
          uncontrollably,'

Before returning to senses. My father said to me, 'You answer
As if you are speaking on the radio,' and it was true. Records say

On February 5, 1988 we 'went to sleep at 3:45 in the morning,' Father
'Feeling tired, with a pain in his heart.' Snow fell, an angel dragging light.

*

Twenty-five years have passed. This morning snow arrives like butterflies.
I see us in our small kitchen that first night, standing around each other,
Not knowing what to say. The image disappears into thousands of pages.
I no longer remember the pain in my father's heart. It was long ago.

Geneva, February 28, 2013

Releasing the porcelain birds

I found her porcelain birds today: three in one room,
Eight in the other, and those brought back to my mind
The one with the broken wing my sister and I once fixed

With Mother's nail polish and a matchstick.
The one bird with a broken neck Loredana and I hid
In the dog's cage outside, not to make her angry.

This is only a house inventory by meticulous
Investigators: 'porcelain figurines,' they say,
'An elephant, a lion, a little girl with two puppies,'

And the birds, still around the ballerina,
Among the 'crystal glasses and champagne flutes,'
The 'bottle of Slivovitz' (my parents' glamorous marriage),

Their prized vacuum cleaner, and Bulgarian rose perfume,
My father's 'seven shirts,' 'two colorful ties,' their
'Tape recorder MK235 automatic Grundig made by Unitra Poland.'

'A black table with intertwined vine design,' and again
'Three porcelain figurines (birds),'
'A wall library with two drawers and display case,'

'2 (two) hats made of light fabric and one leather hat,'
'3 (three) man suits,' 'a thick short coat,'
'4 (woman) summer dresses,' 'a violin and a guitar.'

My mother loved porcelain birds;
They must have made her think of flying
When such thoughts were banished

By men with keys to our house,
Who chained her husband to the walls of prisons,
Because his mind escaped to freedom.

'He represents a danger to our state,' a file says:
'Use all methods to monitor her, including special methods.'
'A radio Selena, a radio Gloria,' 'display case with books for reading.'

*

How far you travelled, my still swans, my white sparrows,
Archived for thirty years all over the country, shelved and cleared;
I see you now, when I am too old to take you in my hands

And run with you around the rooms of the house, or
Place you on tree branches to see what the singing birds
Make of you, to mend you when you shatter: as I did long ago.

A birthday letter

The words 'the source informs you' echo in my head
that *other* voice—familiar, comfortable almost,

lining our private cries: 'the inmate wrote'
to his wife and children 'from the Aiud prison.'

Our letters journeyed through the clay-like
maze of secret police desks. Stamps, checks, dates,

signatures indicate officers and places. The paraphrase
of ongoing pain—half the time they paraphrased us.

That voice in introductions sticks to our words
like a skin disease impossible to cure. But then

some sentences from us burst free perhaps because
they're not translatable, editable, condensable.

They stand out in quotation marks:
unexpected missing heartbeats.

On 4 May 1985 my father thought about his birthday:
'Make a cake with fifty candles and take a picture.'

I recall the cake on our kitchen table,
and thinking about him in chains that day.

'My dear, the children are healthy,' Mother said.
'Come to see me with my children,' he said.

'Do you remember me coming home with snow
on my brow?' 'Children, I so much miss you,

I kiss you all and your mother.' And me:
'How beautiful it would have been for you to have been here too!'

'Sell everything you can,' he urged, 'send the children to school.'
'Do not despair, I might be coming home soon.'

We hung onto those few words that could cross
the clay-like murky territories between us.

These letters were like skin that covered
and protected our bodies from the cold outside,

each word a capillary that carried and supported
the life in each one of us. Each word was limitless,

clothed our souls and warmed against despair,
shielded us from *their* world of terror,

transported chills, shivers, anger, warmth
from us to Father, and back from him to us:

they took us to each other as we were.
When the censor took our words and talked *about* them,

discarded our handwriting and wrote *his*,
he became a flaying instrument.

Letters we sent were not received
(until now, thirty years on).

We, Marsyas the Satyr tied to our tree.
The Censor scraped at capillaries of our words,

what survives is howling: 'A year has passed with no news
from you;' 'Something awful is happening to you;'

'No one looks after us anymore, they're all busy;'
'Mother is ill and short tempered, even Grandmother has left;'

'It's disgraceful that you have nothing to eat.'
Thirty years have gone and we have lived

with exposed wounds, doubts, fears, uncertainties.
Now I find the family letters from back then

in the midst of thousands of records.
I reconstruct the way we used to speak,

the way skin used to feel when it was still alive.
Denatured letters in the handwriting of the censor.

*

I make out capillaries under the flaying instrument,
I reconstruct parts of the skin from the words

that were copied out. We now know
what has been taken from us, and how

words alone saved us then
and bring joy now, the joy of finding them,

for in their frail syllables I recognize the old self.
Apollo has cleaned his instrument and left.

'BUTNARU'
at the visit with his daughter

The slash of sliding glass on glass at the window, as
the guard prepared the microphone between us, when
my breath went from my room to his: *another* visit

comes to mind, but not *this* when I said that life is hard,
no wood for winter, no one to help,
school year finished well, and I aim to go to University.

This is a memory I no longer have:
aged seventeen, gone to prison to see my father;
all on my own, Mother was ill.

The transcript says the obj. (my father) rejoiced
in my visit—'the audience with his daughter'—he
asked for news from home, then told me his.

Father said (they say) was ill with nerves but
calming down lately, asked for medicines, and then
announced that in the autumn he might come home.

He charged me with looking after Mother,
my little brother, and working my hardest at school:
things will become easier, when he returns.

*

Even today I do not dare ask him how
it felt then to look through the glass wall
and see a kind of freedom on the face of his child.

Two days on trains from our village to Aiud,
I wish I could remember what I thought,
if I was afraid to make the trip alone,

and how I felt about leaving him in that glass room
with his feet and hands in chains, my head full
of news to bring home to my ailing mother.

*

A quarter of a century without memory of this visit?
Now the handwriting of the officer on duty
calls me to the transcript with my name on it—daughter

of a convict with a code-name: my grandfather's name
to be exact, probably used as mnemonic device
that linked us through generations across the country.

The record remembers what I no longer keep
in a self that I half-made with forgetting. Now the struggle
is between me and a piece of paper that talks about a girl.

*

The visit closes once again, dear life. I pray:
let it be as tender this time too, no crying, no hysterical
emotions, just pushing on and getting through.

And yet. Here's my father framed in his jailer's words,
our private sorrows like those of characters in plays:
at once my life, and so removed from me.

My father, his jailer, and I, a fine triangle.
Time on my side, I fling this stone of (rescued?) memory
into the river where you cannot step twice.

Transcribed from the Romanian Language

POST: 13JDER
No. Files: 2
NO: 0026124

STRICTLY SECRET
EXEMPLARY UNIQUE
DATE: 26.10.1988
INDICATIVE: 1/B.I.

Exploitation [illegible]
'Barbu'

Hour 5:50 obj. and wife leave for work. At hour 18:10
wife returns to domicile. After 25 min. arrives also
the obj. In the room we record the following discussion:

Wife: Where did you go?

Obj.: At Saftica. She will come by tonight. Everywhere
I went I was asked which roads I take when I return
home. By the railway tracks or by the main road, and
what route I take to go to work.

Wife: Oh, you don't say!?

Obj.: I will go to Samoila (his boss at work) and I
will explain this, and I will come home with the 5:30
(17:30?). What am I to understand from this?

Wife: Only that they want to 'plan' something for you?

Obj.: If they want to 'plan' something, why should they
spread the rumours all around? To 'plan' something, you
work quietly..

Wife: This is so they learn your routes.

Obj.: To find this out, they could snoop around for a
week and…

Wife: Of course, you can only take this road to the
railway station.

Obj.: This is to terrorize me. That's what I suspect.

Wife: Yes, so you find out.

Obj.: Yes, so I will 'be afraid'. That's what I think.
If they wanted to do something, they wouldn't 'talk'.
[…] Maybe they want to get some hooligans to beat me.

Wife: Yes.

Obj.: They can bring their hooligans from Bucharest,
theirs.

Wife: From today onwards we go together to the railway
station. When you return from work, you walk with
Balasa and I wait for you. Did you also tell Sofica
about this?

Obj. Yes.
(. . .)

Their way

They are both old now, Dad turned seventy-nine,
I knew them mostly fighting with each other,
bickering like kids at school, playing tough.

How could I have guessed 26 October 1988
when she'd asked him where he'd been
and he replied, 'Everywhere I went

I was asked which way I take when I return home,
by the railway tracks or by the main road,
and what route I take to go to work.' 'Oh, you don't say,'

she said. 'This is to terrorize me. That's what I suspect.'
'From today onward we go together to the train station,'
she then said. What did she plan to do? Defend him

from murder with her own body? Shelter him from thugs?
They don't know I read this record, a quarter century on:
I am the link between their hearts, taking Love home

the way of words rescued from the state archives:
against forgetting, and against their silly parents' fights.
She stood sentinel for him at the station—and 45 years of marriage.

At hour 1:32

'At hour 1:32 we could hear someone trying the door that leads to the room equipped with listening devices.'

We always pretended to sleep, breathed regular deep breaths—as much as we could force ourselves—when their key clicked in our door.

'The door did not open, after which we could hear the footsteps of someone going away, and the insistent barking of the dog as to a person who is a stranger to the house.'

After they left, we collapsed in leaden sleep. We woke up in the mornings with our heads pounding hearts tired of racing through the night, drank our linden tea in silence.

Then Father would take the hatchet from behind the stove and patrol the house 'This is my house, no one comes into my house, or I'll kill him!' He'd wait with our key placed in the door, so it couldn't be pushed out.

*

That's how he remained in my mind: guarding the door
from the inside, dog outside, poised to cry for help
to deaf neighbors, while shadows of hats and shoulders
crouched along walls for as long as nights lasted.

Transcribed from the Romanian language

POST: 13 I.D.E.R.
No. Files 1
No: 0026124

Strictly Secret
Ex. Unique
Date:23.02.1988
INDICATIVE 1./ B.I.

BARBU

At hour 22.00 the objective listens to the news trans-
mitted by the post 'Radio Free Europe'. His wife is busy
knitting. At hour 22:25 the objective attempts to put
Catalin to bed, by telling him a story with something
imaginary, the action taking place in the West, with a
life of plenty and without worries, a country with lemon
and orange trees..

Wife: . . . It's good also here with apples, and pears and
prunes..

Obj.: . . . I have been reading the magazine The World
and saw that 'there' in the developed countries the
food problem is something entirely banal, everything
is easily available . . . So where is it better? There,
where you can find a piece of good cheese, or here with a
piece of hard black bread?

Wife: Also here is good!...

24.02.88
Transcribed: T.G.

'There'

The boy was five years old and he trusted
his father's stories about a life of plenty,

a country with lemon and orange trees.
'It is something imagined,' the records say.

'Apples and pears and prunes are also good,'
the mother countered (for the microphones?)

no doubt, tired of the hard black bread
the husband-prisoner brought to her.

But he went on imagining the blooms of
orange groves, endless summer trips

we were to take if not for real,
then in his stories with the action

taking place in the West,
itself a forbidden word

those days when we secretly cherished
his unstoppable, rambling dream.

I sat in silence weighting apples, pears, and plums
against mesmerizing gallops across distant prairies.

Transcribed from the Romanian Language

POST: 13 JDER
No. Files: 1
No. 26124

Strict Secret
Exemplary Unique
Date: 24.10.1988
Indicative: 1/B.I.

'Barbu'

27.10.1988
Report urgently to direction to include these aspects
[signature illegible]

Hour 5:17 the objective's entire family wakes up. Among the recorded conversations, the obj. tells Carmen:

'You must be very careful because you will be followed.'

Carmen: I don't care. If I could have been your lawyer at your trial, I would have saved you from going to prison.

Obj.: I see. So you also understood that I served time in prison for nothing.

Carmen: Of course.
[. . .]

Transcribed: P.A.
26.10.1988

October 26, 1988

According to the record number zero-zero
twenty-six-thousand-one-hundred-and-twenty-four,

that morning I woke up at five-seventeen and
made an affirmation that stirred police to action.

The conversation took place at post 13 JDER,
number of files 1, strict secret, only one record of it kept,

for the attention of 1/B.I. In other words
I was at home with my brother, sister, and my parents.

Were there really twenty-six thousand plus records
on us the year before we left the country?

There are *arrows* that mark my words:
I said to my father that I would have saved him

from going to prison if I could've been his lawyer,
he warned me about being tracked by them.

He seemed surprised I understood he served
for nothing, and sure of myself I let the 'Of course,' slip.

To find such a record shining from the litany of blame
which then seemed just and also safe as self-defence.

Preparing for the journey of return
For Catalin

Do you remember the house, I asked my brother,
he was six and a half when we had left.

The grape vine trellis, he said, leading to the garage,
the right turn on the path toward the front door, the porch.

Are you afraid of what we'll see when we get there,
I asked my sister, and she said, yes, of the unknown,

because we're going where we haven't gone before:
inside our father's prisons, we'll see what no child should see.

Mother, I asked, since we left together we fought
illness and separation, loneliness and fears,

and we have embraced new languages,
starting from nothing in the middle of our lives.

Do you think this journey back will take us full circle,
will we find our old selves in our old house, do you

sense our roots pulling us back to the village soil?
It will be good to say good-day in our language, she said,

I miss the people and old streets, but home is now here;
today I cleared the yard and burned the leaves.

I asked my father, what about you, what will we find in prisons?
Suffering bathed in blood he said. And at home, suffering bathed in tears.

And so we start from two continents, suitcases made and locked,
me with the maps of failure and dreams, rescued from police archives.

October 2013 – February 2014

The prisoner-scribe's allowance

Walls are manuscripts and finished books, illuminated
With what the poet found in his cell: words of prayer
Snagged around the throats of rats, weaving the soul

With the spider's net, working its way in the darkness,
By the boarded window that only serves to remind him
Of the sky and air he could not let himself dream for.

Beware the dreams inside those rooms, they spring at you
For a clean kill: 'Punishment must be like this,' my father said,
'After all, you tried to change a country; don't dream in there.'

The guards do not give the prisoner-scribe a pen: that would
Turn the scribe into a man. He is left alone with the walls.
But what riches those walls, the souls of others spilled

Out on their cement face, their ghosts dancing in the shadows
Of the scribe's mind, material for books, four canvases wide open!
And forty-five kilograms of chains to turn into writing instruments:

The rust, the dried blood, here's the ink. He chooses the wall
By the invisible window and begins to write with the links of the chains
Moving his body around, etching the letters into the cement,

Until the first line comes out: 'Our Father who art in Heaven!'
He looks at his work, he has written over someone else's line—
He writes between another's lines, 'Hallowed be Thy Name.'

And beside another's, 'Thy Kingdom Come.'
Then he illuminates the manuscript, now his nail is the pen,
Ink the blood on his knuckle, he is instrument.

October 2013 – January 2014

March 20, 1965:
File of Certification for Transfer of Objects

The undersigned Lieutenant Colonel Cantaragiu Zehtin
of Military Unit 02866 Constanta handed in, and Major
Apostol Ion from the Regional Section M.A.I. Dobrogea,
received the following documents and objects:

1). 1 (one) protocol (certificate) of area search
comprising two files and an appendix of 4 (four)
photocopies;
2). 1 (one) tourist rucksack;
3). 1 (one) binocular case;
4). 2 (two) woollen blankets;
5). 1 (one) shaving razor;
6). 1 (one) shaving brush;
7). 1 (one) shaving paste;
8). 1 (one) battery 4.5W;
9). 1 (one) lighter;
10). 1 (one) coin of 3 lei;
11). 4 (four) coins of 1 leu;
12.) 6 (six) coins of 5 bani;
13.) 2 (two) coins of 10 bani;
14.) 1 (one) English-Romanian dictionary;
15.) 1 (one) German textbook-12 pages long, in
deteriorated state;
16.) 3 (three pieces of cotton for wrapping the feet);
17.) 1 (one) beer bottle that contains 50 ml of medical
alcohol;
18.) 17 (seventeen) half-slices of hunters' salami;
19.) 2 (two) thin loaves of bread;
20.) 1 (one) screwdriver.

The aforementioned objects belong to escapees Bugan
Ion and Petrica Tudor who crossed the frontier from the
Popular Republic of Romania to the Popular Republic of
Bulgaria on the day of 21.02.1965 hours 23:35 between
the points 110-111.

No objections were made to this transfer.
Concluded today 20.03.1965 in Constanta.

From the UM 02866 Constanta
Lt. Colonel, ss/Z.Cantaragiu

From the Dobrogea regional branch M.A.I.
Ss/Mr. Apostol Ion

A walk with my father on the Iron Curtain

Arm in arm, my father and I return
to the ground of his failed escape:
it is now forty-eight years on.

The border between Romania
and Bulgaria at 110-111 point
is bathed in gold October light.

The maize silos where he slept are still here:
an old border guard curious to see us
loitering on the train tracks confirms Dad's memory,

as if History itself sent him our way
with the flock of geese and the red tractor
raising all the clamor in the peaceful morning.

It's a holy day for me, at my father's side,
with the map of his life, listening, listening
to the tempest in that night, icy rain, snow,

him and his friend inside the maize shelter
melting snow for tea, the horrifying days
when they searched the way with binoculars.

He ran to the other side of the world
with seventeen half-slices of salami,
a flashlight, and a dictionary,

some coins, probably more for good luck
than for anything they could buy, the shaver
for good looks, and a heart full of hope.

We carry on past Negru Voda:
Tolbukhin railway station, golden afternoon
and a wind that buffets us,

then Elhovo that looks more like a painting
with a dream worked inside the peeling blue
walls of the train station, my father, a puzzle

in changing light, seen through broken windows,
the coffee and baklava on the main street.
Arm in arm in the old quarters searching for the hotel

where he hid from police, the trap door that is
no longer there. Memory leads us off the map.
Then Lesovo in fog, like an elusive fish, the map

with the haystack where he slept to hide
from border guards, his hike along the roads
through the circular swamp, 400 meters from Turkey!

Ground of being on his ground of escape.
You cannot take the dreams away from anyone who dreams.
'I never thought I'd be back here as a free man,' he says.

Here he is, the white in his hair, snowbells at temples,
the grey-green eyes, now wet, now dry, twinkling.
Locals watch us step off ghost trains at the disused station.

The house founded on elsewhere

He who turns against his language, adopting that of others, changes his identity and even his deceptions. He tears himself—a heroic betrayal—from his own memories, and up to a point, from himself.

Emil Cioran, from *The Temptation to Exist*
(translated from Romanian by Carmen Bugan)

I.
Today is allowed to exist and then vanish
Like the seagulls and their shadows on
The still-seeming water in the Bay of Bantry,

Where I walk unnoticed, unrecorded,
Making memories of compass jellyfish swimming
Up with the tide, after the storm, to the beach.

My own shadow, stooping, standing
Over rocks and sand, back on the walking path,
Simply means that I exist, and there is light.

That is all that will remain of today, no official record
Will testify against what I say that I see. As for me,
I hover in the space between the seagull and its shadow

Loose like a thought that tries to cling to something,
To celebrate the swans and their mirror image,
That medusa that opens like a flower in the sun,

Green lobster nets and masts of boats
Writing something oracular on the horizon
For those who are without a home.

II.
The first crack appeared on the ceiling:
Thin like the shadow of a spider's thread
Cast along the crease where the walls merge.

No one other than her noticed it there.
She couldn't take her mind off it, the way it
Stood in her view as she looked out at mountains

Between trees from her place at the table:
It brought a subtle wrinkle on her face.
Later on a larger fissure appeared, the paint

Swelled like the skin below the eye following
Sleepless nights, plain to see above the table.
She set to mixing cement, took out

Smoothing instruments, drained the weeping wall
And mended until all looked well again.
She built the new house with words bought

At the price of exile, letting memories go astray,
Fall where they may like dust.
How many times she walked around the rooms

Anxious and proud that she made it all with a translated
Prayer, a new version of the old prayer, holy
Oil from elsewhere, rituals and superstitions

From elsewhere, but all renewed and changed
Again, four languages over, where they show
Why they could pass through words that changed her.

III.
When the walls became full of cracks she knew no words
She cemented would last unless she uncovered
The foundation of elsewhere on which her house was built.

She dug around it, moved the earth little by little until the old stones
Showed through: porous pain, old fears, mistrust. She placed
Next to them what she could find around: a bit of happiness, a bit of fear

A little bit of courage. All in the language where she
She learned them. Cement now, water, patience,
Piece by piece the foundation is renewed.

She looks at her children and husband. She will mend this wall
With words from here and elsewhere and let them
Help her build, rebuild, and fix: their common love and skill

Should outlast time, be stronger than her will alone.
They play-build like when she was young and poured the foundation
Of that first house she cannot forget: the childhood house of joy.

IV.
Stefano is three years old, he fills his shirt with pears
And runs: 'Mommy look, what shall we do with them?'
I take out the camera and rush to him, his soft cheeks,
Busy little hands, his golden curls. The grass is full of pears.

V.
Alisa puts her arms around me: 'Come play with me!'
She runs around the room with her bare little feet, here, there,
Like a sunray that escapes through wind-blown trees
In summer's day, and lights up unexpected places.

VI.
It is the lucid sky after the wind
Has swept the debris that has come from far away:

Cirrus clouds like torn night shirts,
On the shoulder of the Jura whitened with first snow.

All clean now wherever you look, lit by the coin of the moon.
Turning to the second half of life,

Knees grazed against the web of splintered light.
And here it comes, a word at work through those fallen notes:

The touch that brings on all other touches
With the rightness in them, turning and moving again with you,

The moonlight sonata in my ears in morning sun at the desk:
Different this time, a new kind of music, awake, luminous.

VII.
Not all the words you say are the Self and not all turning
Against your language is self-betrayal. Behind each word
Is what tries to get inside it. That is what matters

Whether I speak it in my own language,
Or in the tongue of others. The thought, the breath
With which you send love out, or forgiveness, say,

Outlive the words and languages, outstrip
The syllables at prayer or play. I speak of smiles and tears,
And better yet, smiles through tears at the end of day.

And so the house stands with what it can:
A sagging wall, a brand new door through which
Come children with schoolbooks and street-side flowers;

Solid enough to face the winter wind and baking heat,
Each word inside for what it's worth and what it can say:
Good enough to bear the weight of what's to come.

June 18 – July 10, 2014

Morning walk with Rosa

In memory of Jon Stallworthy who nurtured till the end

You have to be there at the moment when
The sun works with the milk-thick fog
And both of them are paper-white light.

Things as they are no longer seem the same,
You stand in the field, inside the foot of a rainbow
Looking at fog lifting through the rising sun.

Millions of glistening droplets float by
Leaving your cheeks wet, hair humid,
And your breath snagged on a 'spider-made-star'

As Rosa whispers, 'étoile.' So that is what's under the fog:
Spider-made stars. Perfectly symmetrical webs
Of fine silk-like threads hanging on blackberry bushes,

Late pink baby roses, between leaves of trees,
From stem to stem and every branch. And now
The sun turns slightly golden and I see

Delicate parachutes landed between ravaged
Sunflowers' stalks, domes of white sky-light
As if the field is lit up by a thousand white lamps.

The spiders have worked with the fog: their nets
Are clad in tiny droplets, minuscule pearls, diamonds,
Disciplined, in perfect rows hanging to the threads

That have followed the shapes of leaves, for now
We are looking at trampolines made of spider webs
Drizzle-plaited, finished off with pyramid-like tops,

And here come the double, triple layered iridescent sheets
Of honey-comb-like structures swaying to our breaths.
Then back to spider-made-stars

That flutter in the air holding their glitter
Up in the open fields, half green, half brown.
I have never seen so many nets carrying water light.

October weaves her tapestry on grasses,
Nets on trees, and we run fingers along translucent
Threads to collect the water on our skin,

Touching the miraculous. So much to see
In the fog, as in the last days' sadness.
The richness that's around seems deeper

When you didn't know to look for it, and saw it there
As fog's offering – a path full of shimmering stones
To help you find your way when you can't see ahead:

The spider web that hangs to the mailbox
Drawing your mind away from the letter,
Into its calming inner architecture

That depends on just one kind of warmth
Born of a sudden morning chill that makes the vapor rise
From mounds of leaves, and fog breathes rainbows.

*Here, 'etoile', star, is playing with misunderstanding of the French 'toile d'araignée'

October 14 – November 12,
Prevessin–Vesgnin–Ornex–Moens

Crossing the woods with Dennis

It's eight-thirty on a September morning and he stands by the front door next to Martine and Rosa, waiting for me with his walking stick, sunglasses, and the instrument that will measure the time and distance we will make today; trajectory, the natural reserve of Meyrin, ancient village of Mategnin, sunflower and cornfields on the border between France and Switzerland leading to the woods and farms between the checkpoints.

This is one of my favorite walks for it zigzags inside the thickness of the border and we always go without passports, being what we are: *frontaliers*, creatures of frontiers, carrying earth from one country to another on the soles of our shoes. He stops at all the mud puddles in the woods to look for frogs with his stick, and moves easily along the deer paths as if he were a hunter. They all discuss which way avoids the roads, the best lane to the farm that sells asparagus, they taste peas in a field.

We wander under the canopy of arches deep into the woods that lead to fallen trees, and thick thickets, magical and quiet as if no one ever walked into them. The air is opulent with leafy smell, humid earth, clearings release grassy sun-warmed currents that go up my arms making me giddy. Then comes Mategnin around the bend of a road lined with sycamores: first a farmhouse restored, a huge garden with strayed-about white chairs and geranium pots spread on lush grass. The village fountain where we drink above a rectangular stone vase from the mouth of an iron lion, and then the village green, a small circle around one tree with two benches under it. That's all Mategnin is, about seven-eight houses that were kept with all the ancient stone in them and have geraniums on all the small square windows peering out into green fields.

On the way home, through the village of Prevessin, Dennis looks at houses and points to his wife, Rosa, those he'd like for himself: the one with the wood for burning stacked all around the walls, or the one with the antique cart (as in horse-drawn cart) near the swimming pool, which, he observes, is well-placed behind the rosebush hedges, so it looks like a lake. Or the big house that would have place for his whole family, his mother too, who scolds him for reaching beyond his means, though he doesn't really crave the richness of those mansions, he only dreams aloud to pass the time. And so we're on our way. My jacket pockets are full of walnuts Rosa gathered from the walk and offered as a gift; a gift of the road, the three of them richer than they will ever know.

Through the village streets

For Stefano

All of a sudden it seems you read:
The street sign that we passed by all these years ago
Today says in your boy's voice,
Fin de zone 30, Prevessin–Moens,
Our street opens up to you the rights-of-ways.

Your hand is nearly as big as mine now;
We exchange gloves to mock the winter wind,
And you leave messages for me written in
Letters that straggle off the words like children
Standing in a crooked line. You read what I write—

A hurried letter (Dear Lucy…) stealing that silence
From me, when I am alone with the paper.
Suddenly it seems, you read,
And I remember your first smile drunk in breast-milk,
The moment when you looked into my eyes,

The first time when you recognized me in a crowd,
That one day when you laughed for the first time
Because something was funny, and we wrote it down
So you can find it later, when you're grown.
But now you read, and with you I take all words as true.

Is this window ours?

For Stefano

Which window? I ask holding his hand
As we walk the length of our rented apartment.
'This one that looks at the mountain,' he says
And then turns, 'And this wall, Mummy, is it ours?'

'Nothing is ours,' I smile to him, myself
Now used to the sunny almost empty rooms,
That we un-cluttered in order to make more space
For him to breathe better.

We play this game so often, and when he asks me
To buy the whole apartment, with walls and windows,
The light bulbs and the cupboards, I don't know
What to say, except, 'There will be other windows

That will show us other things, don't worry about owning
One. In having none we have all of them:
Like countries and like languages.' 'Yes, Mummy,' he says,
'But I like this one, can we choose this one?'

New Poems

(2016-2019)

And now, the words

I struggle with the meaning of the word *resurrection*:
Go do your work, word, I say,
All the way back to your root. Then return to me
To stand by these children fished out of the luminous sea
So that I could see your face
In horrified eyes, not saved, but filled with almost-life.

I used to be *resurgere,* rise again, the word says
Sounding like rain on my grandparents' house.
Remember, it says, dragging your refugee self
Out of the rumble of trains at Roma Termini,
And wanting to once again be free:
These children rise out like admonitions.

I try to remember when the word arrived to me,
From whose mouth, or whose book I'd learned it,
And memory obeys: childhood Easter, Resurrection Mass
With a trail of candles in the night: *Invierea, Veniti sa luati lumina.*
Coming back to life, come take light. But these children
Fished out of the ancient Mediterranean:

This is my lifetime, resurrection, I say, look how they
Swim away from the cataclysm of war, I see them
Pulled out of water, as if they are being lifted
Into afterlife. Yet this is our life, is this what you mean
To me, in my lifetime, word? Shame burns
On their blue faces, bright like swords.

Put me next to the children, the word says, and I shout:
Resurrect Children. The present opens:
There is no hell but here, no heaven but here--
Their indicting eyes will never leave us.
Here they are before me this Sunday morning, born
On the horizon of nightmare, reaching out with their tiny hands.

New life

By the time she reached the age of twelve,
The girl with the red scarf and brown eyes
Had seen human body parts scattered in front
Of the house where she had been born, and she had
Fallen asleep to the sound of bombs and rifles.

She had walked out of the ruins of her own house,
Crossed eight countries, mostly on foot,
Scaling snowy mountains, descending on railway tracks
To signal the way to her parents who pushed the pram:
Made her own map of this world.

Through the nets of barbed-wire fences,
Cataloguing, as she passed through, the beatings
Her parents suffered at the borders where they crossed,
She looks back and smiles at the words
She has now abandoned, because they no longer help.

At her first school, the teacher speaks a language of freedom
Unknown to her. In this new language, she says
She'd like to plant a garden with her parents and her brother,
Who tries his own language as he sits up in the pram, rattling
A plastic toy donated to him by a benevolent woman.

The map of the world the girl has drawn
Is being absorbed by the map of this century—
Soles of shoes scattered across the way to hope.
The road to a better life has not yet been planned,
Everyone is waiting for an architect.

Piano

for Alisa and Stefano

It was perfectly tuned.
I first saw it by the railing
that overlooked the pond
filled with white and red
water lilies and red fish.

I had never played the piano,
so the first time I sat on the chair,
under the thick willow,
with the sun streaming
through the leaves
making patters on the keys,
I looked around to make sure
no one could hear me.

And then I tried out notes till I fell
in a sort of trance with the wind rustling,
the pond lapping, and the scales
dispersing into the greenery.

To my right, beyond the keys,
the fish gathered at the edge of the pond,
under the boardwalk. Hundreds of them,
like a red, shimmering belt.

That afternoon, when my children
returned home from school, I took them
to the piano and they invented a duet.
They were biting their lips gently--
there was a feeling of life in their faces
that I will never forget.

People came by, curious.
Some knew how to play and delighted

in showing off their skills.
Others stood by listening.

It was as if the piano had always
been there and everyone
stopped by to play a tune—
their baguettes and bottles of wine
in bags at their feet.

When we left the country it was winter,
the piano was no longer there,
but by then everyone
knew each other, so they made
music with their friendly chatter
by the frozen pond.

Boy playing the cello
For Stefano

The chair he sits on is two hundred years old;
It modulates like the voice of his grandfather

Welcoming him to sit on his lap.
He straightens his back holding the cello

As if they're old friends. The two are about the same size.
This tree was chosen to make a different kind of music

From that of rain and wind that fell on its leaves,
Or from the dry woodpecker knock, the scratching

Claws of squirrels up and down its bark, branches and twigs,
The song of cardinals, robins and blue jays darting back and forth.

The boy holds the cello in his arms. His eyes are full of music,
Dreamy with notes about to happen, and the bow lies near

Like a promise of a journey. When he begins to play,
I think the heart of the tree gladdens in the dry,

Sunny house, giving into memories that long for summer
Thunderstorms, dawn choruses, in a low, echoing sound.

The wood, transformed, returns to its essence,
As the boy brings the marvelous into the house.

Black Sea memories

I felt it was restraining what it holds within,
All spread out and calm-looking
In her bed of grasses and dunes, bringing

To our faces a sort of light that made me still:
Blue fingers searched the folds of autumn sand,
Its surge convinced caresses through the rocks.

My body gave into it, breath first, the water
Behind my eyes called to its salt and memory:
Feeling again that fear of immensity.

If you could admit that the shallow breath
Of the waves could draw you in, until you lost
Footing and skill, when it's too late to refuse

Its embrace, the strength of it that suffocates.
You too trusted and touched that blue shirt, the face
That smiled in the sun, and turned away from you with you in it.

Long Island Sound

January 9, 2018

It was as if breath itself was missing—
Gone the brine and gulls and rush of water
On frozen sand. I walked on the tip of a wave
Scanning for the ribbon of water near horizon.

Waves crashed in memory while I crumbled
Their unnatural lift frozen on the gasp,
Exposed in their nothing-saying.
I stood on frozen movement, praying,

To see again that which I knew and cherished:
The translucent lift of water and algae,
Clam shells and egg-like rosy stones,
Fluent ending in a new beginning.

Christmas 2017

I see the tumour wrapped around my father's aorta like a link in a chain. It cannot be touched by knife or radiation. It cannot be touched at all. It must not be disrupted or disturbed. Here he is sitting next to my brother beside the Christmas tree with a present from us. And here he is coughing in the night, giving me the same feeling I have when my son coughs in the night from asthma. I cannot make myself think. What is left of his hard life? How do I take this last part of the journey with him? His cough and my breath.

My sister's tumor is deep into her breast, too close to the lungs. Every morning at 10 she receives a dose of radiation and every morning I pray it will not scatter into her lungs, into her heart. Her girls are the age of my children. Here we are at Christmas sleeping together in the same bed, like when we were girls. She takes off her shirt and shows me the radiation tattoo, the bruises from the surgeries. You can see through fear as through clear water. I hold her when she falls asleep. She holds me when I turn in bed, unable to sleep. There she is doing cartwheels in our first house, thumping on the sacred, welcoming ground of our country, which had later become the betraying ground of our country.

The earth has shifted from under us many times. But we remained together, suspended in the air, like words, linked.

An old woman reading

One story ends and another opens on sunlit pages.
Though her arms seem burdened with the heavy book,
She is entirely inside the words, oblivious

To pain or being painted, her cloak the color
Of a red giant star, or the edges of planetary nebulae.
Rembrandt must have enjoyed their mutual silence

As he poured earth from Siena with his hands
Over the granite table, mixing it with linseed oil
And his spatula, patiently waiting for her

To go into the chapters.
The Belgium heart stone looks grey-black;
You must grate the oil-soaked earth into granite

With its wide top: the top of the heart.
Some say she must be Hannah the Prophetess.
Then she must read about Time, and how

We are made of earth, for here
Is made of earth, oil, and stone. Breathing
Woman, image, story in painted earth.

*

The sun this morning shines through
Rembrandt's windows into his studio filled
With shells, heavy catalogues, philosophers' heads.

His old woman shall forever read in her frame
And we, of earth but not yet back into it,
Eat its other offerings prepared by a chef from far away:

Bright green wild pepper leaves
Sprinkled with roasted coconut and peanuts, lime and ginger,
Red onion, chili, dried shrimp doused in secret honey.

We taste the earthiness of his homeland
From his hands, which fold the wild pepper leaves.
He feeds us his fare, gratefully.

His hands are old as hers, the skin under his chin
Sags like hers, but his house is fragrant. He touches us
The way she touches our minds—her shawl in embers,

And a sun that illuminates the book
Wider than her lap, opened to a space between
Chapters: out of timelessness and back.

Penn Station, NY, January 23

He must be about eighty years old
And looks glad for the warmth
Of the crowded corridors filled with smells
Of food, luggage, and strong perfume.

He sits at the next table holding a garbage bag,
Takes out a box at a time, a wrap at a time,
Licks the crumbs, and makes a pile of paper
Next to his right hand. Some seaweed, a bite

Of rice fallen from a sushi, a piece of noodle.
No one minds him, they look at their boxes
Filled with raw fish and ginger, check their phones,
The music from the restaurant plays on.

He smells like garbage. His eyes are warm
And resigned, but the crumbs make a meagre meal,
So, when he finishes going through the wraps,
He starts all over from the stack of empty boxes,

As if opening them again and again
Will make the food appear, the way we replay
A memory hoping the rehearsal will
Divine a treasured moment, and bring it back.

When he is convinced nothing is left, he carries the stack
To the large bin that had been just emptied.
He takes a napkin from the supply station, returns
To his place at the table, and wipes it clean.

Love

In the morning, when I walk outside,
She is waist-deep in tomato vines
Collecting the first batch in a glass bowl;
Cucumbers hang below yellow flowers,
Purple chili shine from a flat bush
Under green bell peppers.

He takes me by the hand to the garage
Where he now has a fridge, a sink, and a grill
In the place where he used to keep tools.
Three of the walls are still large altars
With the pictures of us children, each one a wall
And a vase of flowers, an icon, or a cross.

He opens a bottle of whisky he had been keeping
For a day just like this, when I might be visiting,
And never mind it's only half past ten, he fills the glasses
With a smile wider than the sunflowers outside the door:
'Oh, come and drink with me, my child,' he says.
Around his aorta, the tumor coils.

Inside his heart there is the cleanest blood,
The pure happiness of being old, at peace
With all that life has offered.
She, five fractured ribs, walks slowly
With the morning's harvest and we light the grill.
She won't drink but will hold a glass

To toast the year's reward: their daughter home.
I walk around the garden with them, taking pictures
Of the willow they had planted the year I married,
Which now shades the entrance, the calla lilies,
Queens of the night and honeysuckle bushes,
Purple pansies and pink mouth-of-the-lion blooms.

And I pray that every full stop I put in these lines
Is in the right place, every comma after the right time
That passes between walking from one flower to another,
While the glasses empty slowly and we are grateful
That we still can have that one drink, together,
Standing in the sunshine, with the song of birds.

Moon

The full sunlit side of the moon filled
Our room with light
That broke through autumn trees;

We could have stayed awake all night trying
To name it, as it lit up the clock, corners,
Our heads on the pillows.

But we fell asleep with its light
On our eyelids, with nothing to hide,
Not even stolen dreams.

I felt not too far from being translated,
The same way sunlight was interpreted
By the moon face we could see.

Rings

The growth rings inside trees cannot lie,
They're like our bones which thicken with years
Of bending over children, grinding the wheat,
'Bone goes through bone,'
Grandmother Floarea used to say.

Tree rings, each cradled in the next,
Each as evidence of what the world has offered
And how the tree has worked with it;
How one grew round the other,
Strengthening the core with its own essence.

And words? Do they grow like the tree rings
From our humanity? *Democracy*, from Socrates
(Who said it contains all of our vices)
To our lifetime when our virtues will not be elected
By our votes. Can we say delusion of freedom?

Grandmother said, 'I work so you will have
An easier life. I grind my bones for you.'
When you fell the tree, to see its growth rings,
You cut off its life. Cut off the freedom to see
How it is made, and you'll stand on a stump.

Plato told the parable of the boat steered
By its passengers: he said democracy doesn't work.
We each take a turn at capsizing our ship
In the still benevolent sea. There will be rings
In the water, where we go down.

CPSIA information can be obtained
at www.ICGtesting.com
Printed in the USA
FFHW021117310719
53968149-59701FF